Inuksuk Journey

Inuksuk Journey

AN ARTIST AT THE TOP OF THE WORLD

MARY WALLACE

MAPLE
TREE
PRESS

Maple Tree Press books are published by Owlkids Books Inc.
10 Lower Spadina Avenue, Suite 400, Toronto, Ontario M5V 2Z2
www.mapletreepress.com

Distributed in Canada by Raincoast Books
9050 Shaughnessy Street, Vancouver, British Columbia V6P 6E5

Distributed in the United States by Publishers Group West
1700 Fourth Street, Berkeley, California 94710

Acknowledgments

Thanks to the Ontario Arts Council, the Alariaq family, the Intven Wallace family, the Super Six family, the family of artists in the Making Art Creating Community program at Museum London, the Kinngait artists, the Raincoast family, and the Maple Tree Press family. Thanks to Pat and Jim Hinds for their traveling company, as well as for their flora photo contributions. Thanks to James Stinson for the artwork photography. And thanks to my sister Liz Kristiensen for her photographs of me.

Cataloguing in Publication Data
Wallace, Mary, 1950-
    Inuksuk journey : an artist at the top of the world / Mary Wallace.

Includes index.
ISBN 978-1-897349-26-7

    1. Wallace, Mary, 1950- –Travel–Canada, Northern–Juvenile literature. 2. Canada, Northern–Description and travel–Juvenile literature. 3. Inuksuit–Juvenile literature. 4. Canada, Northern–In art–Juvenile literature. 5. Canada, Northern–Pictorial works–Juvenile literature. 6. Painters–Canada–Biography–Juvenile literature. I. Title.

Library of Congress Control Number 2008925716

Design & art direction: Word & Image Design
Illustrations: Mary Intven Wallace
Photography: Mary Intven Wallace, except as noted in acknowledgments and polar bears, top right page 29 (iStockPhoto).

We acknowledge the financial support of the Canada Council for the Arts, the Ontario Arts Council , the Government of Canada through the Book Publishing Industry Development Program (BPIDP), and the Government of Ontario through the Ontario Media Development Corporation's Book Initiative for our publishing activities.

ONTARIO ARTS COUNCIL
CONSEIL DES ARTS DE L'ONTARIO

Printed in China

A   B   C   D   E   F

CONTENTS

My Inuksuk Journey

From my first encounter with an inuksuk, stones placed to give a message, I was intrigued. At the time, I had no idea that this ancient Arctic symbol would lead me on an incredibly rich journey across time, place, and culture.

Years later, I found myself on a winter visit to Nunavut, Canada's newest northern territory. I was filled with delight at the many stone messengers I met along the Arctic landscape. My Inuit hosts told me of their many meanings. An inuksuk can mark a family home, welcome guests, guide travelers, and ensure safe passage. Each time I see an inuksuk I feel safe and at one with our land.

This summer I returned to the Arctic to discover what it is like to live in the traditional Inuit way. Instead of winter darkness, I found summer light. The inuksuk was an ever-present guide, showing the importance of friendship, cooperation, and respect.

During our camping trip, my Inuit friends taught me much about what is valuable in life: safety, food, shelter, family, friends, and a sense of awe. I recorded what I saw and felt in my paintings, journal entries, and photographs of the land and people.

Inuksuk Journey is the story of my amazing Arctic adventure.

Day 1: Arriving at the Top of the World

Many hours of travel have brought us high into the Arctic. Our last flight touches down on the southwest coast of Baffin Island. Descending through a foggy layer of clouds, we find ourselves in a land of stone, sea, and sky.

My sister Liz and I have arrived at the tiny oceanside airport in Kinngait (Cape Dorset), Nunavut, eager for our escapade together. We will be living on the land in the way of the ancient peoples of Canada's Arctic. We look around and see men in parkas, women with babies inside their cozy amoutis, and lively, dark-haired children. A friendly face looks up from inside the fur-trimmed hood of her amouti. This must be Kristiina, our hostess. Next to her, a man with bright, dark eyes greets us with a silent shining smile. It's Timmun. They will be our guides.

A Warm Welcome

The chill in the evening air contrasts with the warm welcome we receive. I look out over the endless vast terrain. Everything is unfamiliar. How can anyone survive in this barren place? Standing on pristine tundra, I breathe deeply in the unfamiliar air. Like a stranger on a mysterious planet, I watch a multitude of soft evening colors reflecting all around. Soft pink, brilliant yellow, glistening gold, muted purple, and the deep blue of distant hills shimmer everywhere. Some unknown sea vessels float far off in a frigid bay.

Kristiina and Timmun take us to their home where we meet their extended family of children, in-laws, and grandchildren. Here we meet the young hunter Jamisee, who will also accompany us on our camping trip. Together, we enjoy a delicious dinner of tuktu roast (lean and tender caribou meat), vegetables, and mashed potatoes with lots of gravy. We enjoy a dessert of plump, purple crowberries picked from the surrounding mountains.

Be Prepared

As our evening meal winds down, Liz and I are told that we need to pack for camp. We might be leaving first thing in the morning. We need raingear, bug gear, wind gear, hiking boots, rubber boots, wool socks, several layers of clothing, and a backpack to carry it all in. Weather will vary from very cold to very hot, from freezing rain to burning sun. Kristiina cautions us to dress so that we do not sweat too much; if we do we are sure to be chilled to the bone. Our guides will bring some food, but we will need to hunt. We will be encountering seal, walrus, caribou, and whale on our camping trip. And we are warned about the polar bears, who hunt to kill for their food, and to protect their young.

Filled with information and loaded down with Arctic char (fish) and eggs for breakfast the next day, Liz and I retire to the "beach house," a small wooden structure that sits on a rocky shore overlooking the Arctic Ocean.

I toss and turn that night. "What was I thinking when I brought my little sister here? How will Liz and I survive? Will we have enough food? Can we be safe? What will tomorrow bring? Who will help us? Will we make friends? Why did we come here?" During my long restless night, the day does not get dark. Only eerie twilight waits.

Our guide Timmun.

A beautiful Arctic sunset.

Inuksuk that Welcomes

A noble inuksuk stands in Rankin Inlet as a sign of welcome to this northern Nunavut community.

Telliq Inlet
from above.

Day 2: First Morning

Morning brings brilliant blue skies with layers of fluffy, white clouds. I hear the waves gently lap against the stony Arctic shore. From my bedroom window, I see odd flowers blooming in every shape and hue.

Gazing across the Telliq Inlet at rounded rock hills, we eat our breakfast of smoked Arctic char. A lone inuksuk stands on the highest mountain at the end of an island. It seems to invite us to visit Mallikjuaq. Perhaps today we will discover the secrets of this mysterious place. Sweeping tundra slopes beckon me to uncover unknown stories, written on the land and in stone.

Kristiina goes in her kayak to meet Timmun. I hear the start and stop of the motor of the *Silver Dolphin*, the brand new boat that will transport us across the Arctic Ocean to our summer camping spot. We have already been fitted with survival suits, bright orange bulky snowsuits that we must wear when we travel on the frigid Arctic waters. If we were to fall overboard, the cold water would rapidly paralyze, and then kill us. Our insulating survival gear will give our guides a bit more time to haul us back on board before we succumb.

Not Today

Our hosts let us know that we can not start our sea trip today: maybe tomorrow, maybe the next day. The new boat is not working properly just yet. Kristiina decides that a guide will take us to see the ancient archaeological sites on Mallikjuaq Island instead. She calls over our guide, Pootoogook, who shyly reveals that his name is the Inuktitut word for "Big Toe." He leads us across our bay onto a low-tide land bridge. We face the isolated island place where his ancestors once lived. He carries an oily old rifle. We all know that polar bears are out and about.

We must hurry across while the tide is still low. The icy water is rising fast and will soon cover our path. Pootoogook's knowledge of this puzzling land helps us to feel safe. Above, the circling ravens warn us to be careful as we pick our way over the treacherous boulders, slippery with algae. Just as we reach the shores of Mallikjuaq Island, we look back to see the water washing over our just-walked passageway.

Pootoogook protects us.

My view of the top of the world.

Crossing the Tidal Flats

The view from Kinngait Mountain, overlooking the tidal flats land bridge across Telliq Inlet.

Inuit bone toy.

Looking through the doorway of an ancient Thule home.

Day 2: Ancient Mallikjuaq Island

As we continue our hike along the shore, Pootoogook shares his traditional knowledge of the land of his ancestors. We find out that the first people to live here were the Tunnit (too-neet). Pootoogook explains that archaeologists are still finding Mallikjuaq remains from this culture that dates from 1700 BCE to 1000 AD.

And a second community settled here: the Thule (too-lee) lived here about one thousand years ago, arriving during a three hundred year cycle of warmer weather that allowed sea vessels to reach this shore. During all those years, this seemingly barren and forbidding landscape has offered all the necessities of life, in abundance, to the Inuit and their ancient ancestors.

The natural rhythm of the rocky shore abruptly halts. In front of me is a pile of stones that has not been put there by nature. Peering inside, I glimpse bits of weathered white bones. Looking ahead, I see more strange rocky heaps. What could this be?

The Cache

Pootoogook tells us this series of stone piles are caches built by Inuit hunters of the past. People have been using them here for many years. The rocks covering each cache are large enough so that wolves, foxes, and weasels cannot get in. There are seven caches right here. This is where food is stored, kept fresh in the cold ground near the permafrost, protected from predators by a covering of heavy stones.

I remember hearing a story that says animals came to offer their lives so that the Inuit could live.

The Land Is a Living Whale

There are long, low dark hills ahead. In contrast, a bright white skull shows itself on the beach. "It's from a beluga whale. When someone catches one today, the whole community comes to get a piece. Beluga skin is a delicacy. It is called maktaq," explains Pootoogook.

Pausing, I remember another traditional story I was told. Before time began, the land of the First Peoples was a living whale. To be alive then meant you were connected to everything: past, present, and future. And in this time before time, a community of people here did not have enough to eat. One persistent hunter searched far and wide for food. Finally, he realized that the land was a living whale. He courageously harpooned the whale. Now his people had plenty of food. Also, the whale transformed into land and time as we now know them. This is the reason that Inuit hunters still honor the spirit of the land and the whale today.

As if awaking from a dream, I look up. It seems that the land ahead has taken the shape of a huge whale. I sense the spirits of the ancestors in the darkening sky. Pootoogook tells us a storm is coming.

A beluga whale skull washed up on the beach.

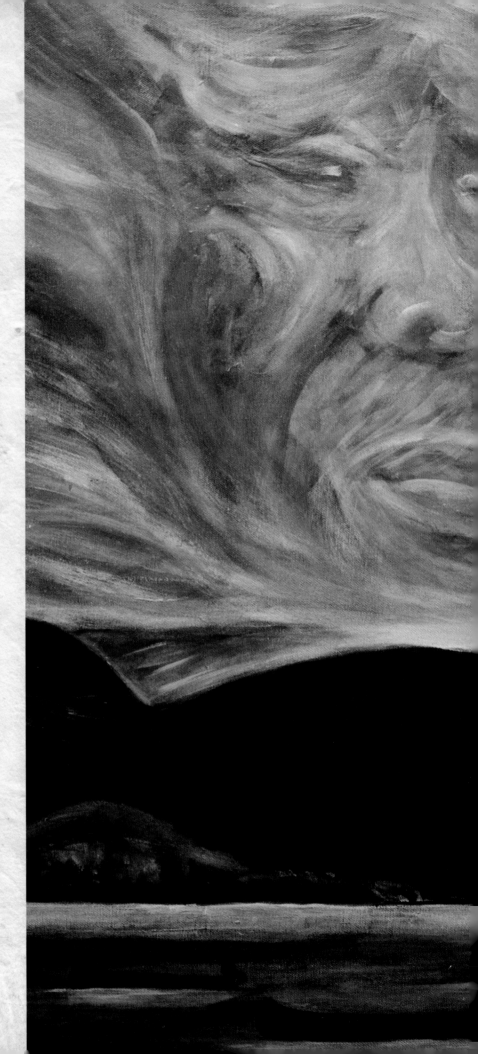

How I Saw the Land

The land of the ancestors
is a living whale.

Day 2: A Trip through Time

*O*ur trio approaches a stone arch that rises from the ground. It appears to invite us in. Entering, we find ourselves inside an ancient Thule winter home.

Pootoogook shows us the entrance, the kitchen, and the sleeping quarters. A giant bowhead whale bone once served as a rafter, supporting a caribou and sealskin roof. We sit down inside the embrace of the circular stone wall. I am where others have lived. Together, our group looks around as we enjoy peeling nibbles of smoked Arctic char from the dried fish skin.

Pootoogook tells us that the elders do not want anything touched or removed from here. There are ancient harpoon heads used for hunting, tools used around the house, tools to make lamps, hunting and cooking tools – everything they had used in those days. He tells us about the living and cooking area in the middle, and the raised sleeping platform at the back. When sleeping, the hunters elevated their feet so they got more strength and energy for hunting and traveling.

A Visit from a Shaman?

Liz and Pootoogook rise and climb out. I remain, drawn to the memory of the people who once gathered here to cook, sew, make tools, and pass the long winter darkness. I imagine a qulliq (soapstone lamp) burning at the

Smoked arctic char.

center, fueled by fat from whales and seals, keeping this home warm despite the freezing cold outside.

Picturing this cozy domestic scene, I suddenly get an impression in my mind of looking through an imagined ice window, and see a fleeting shadow pass. Could this be an ancient shaman – traveling by to ensure that all is well, using magical powers to pass into realms where time does not exist, and to connect past and present? Sensing a great mystery, I slip back into my daydream of a thousand years ago.

Land of Bones

The rustle of a raven's wing startles me back to the present. Giving my head a shake, I stand up and join my hiking companions as they look into the water. Everywhere we see evidence of the life that has been lived here: brown and ocher tools and toys shimmer from below the surface.

There are so many bones lying still in the clear water. Pootoogook points to a bowhead skull, a walrus jaw, and a giant whale vertebra. "There are thousands of bones in this pond. The ancestors threw the bones in the water after they were finished with them. They hunted walrus and whale in skin boats called umiaks and kayaks. Using harpoons and floats, they hunted in the spring and summer Arctic waters, following the floats at the end of their thrown harpoons, often for three or four days, or even a week. Sometimes the boats were tipped over and hunters were lost. They took bowhead whales for food and fuel, making tools and weapons from the whalebone, and nets from the baleen plates from the whales' jaws."

Glancing up, we see that it looks like rain again. Time to head back to shelter for the night.

Thule tools.

An ancient walrus jaw.

Life in Ancient Times

Evidence of lives lived here rests among the stones of an ancient Thule home.

Approaching the family camp.

Day 3: Family Camp of the Ancestors

This morning, Pootoogook shows us the site of his ancestors' family camp. We see the marks left by the ancient peoples: rings of rock that form caches, hunting traps, tent rings, and cairns that cover lost men.

Bits of bone are scattered all around: the remains of whales, caribou, walrus, seals, and rabbits. These animals have shared the land with the Inuit, together here for thousands of years.

As we walk, our footsteps release a fresh tart fragrance into the air from the spongy green moss beneath our feet. Heading towards the ocean, we reach the crest of a tundra trail. A lone inuksuk stands here, silhouetted against the dark sea. As we draw nearer to the shoreline, the inuksuk appears to grow legs, upright arms, and a head, as if saluting us. The lone stone sentinel stands over a stone circle.

Inuksuk that Welcomes

Pootoogook's wife's grandparents lived in this area. We are at the tent ring where they used to set up summer camp. In this place, animals of all sorts were abundant, providing a wealth of food to Inuit families. Delicious meals were shared: food was fresh, frozen, fermented, dried, or cooked. The inuksuk at this campsite was built to let others know that a family lived here. If people traveled and saw this inuksuk, they

knew that someone would be here to provide companion-ship and comfort. Two carefully balanced stone columns next to the tent ring were kayak stands, to keep the kayak out of reach from dogs, who would eat the skin of the boat. Traditional boats were covered in seal skin that dried out and kept its shape. The ribs of the kayak were made of whalebone.

Inuksuk that Warns

Across the Arctic inlet, we spot a rugged point of land jutting into the sea. There stands another inuksuk. It warns of a perilous landing location — the jagged coast is too rough to dare going ashore.

Suddenly, Pootoogook recognizes an irregular speck in the sea. Electrified, he turns to us, "See the bowhead whale breaching in the sea below!" Astonished, we turn and look. There is a disturbance in the water: a large black shape rises from the ocean. Two vapor clouds ascend from the slow-moving mass. The whale is mostly submerged. Then, a large triangular tail fluke emerges, and as it slaps down we glimpse the huge frowning face of a bowhead whale. And just as quickly, it is gone.

It is time to return to Kinngait. We retrace our steps along the rock paths, spotting a single stone inuksuk that shows the safest way home. As we head back, Liz and I wonder if we will leave on our camping trip tomorrow. We are excited at the thought of visiting Inuksuk Point.

A Welcoming Place

Greeted by this golden inuksuk, I know this spot has welcomed people for thousands of years.

Heading to
Fire Pit Mountain.

Day 4: Is it Ice or Is it a Bear?

*Today is the day we finally leave for our camping trip! After a hot breakfast, we go down to the beach to meet Timmun, Kristiina, and Jamisee. The **Silver Dolphin** is finally ship-shape. Jamisee takes us by canoe to board the new boat. In the frosty morning air, wearing survival suits in case we fall into the icy water, we are on our way to the glacial seas.*

The Fire Pit

Skimming over the deep opaque ocean water, we see a breathtaking sight: layers of hills and mountains with inuksuit looking down from the tops. Unexpectedly, an immense stone shape looms ahead — a round mountain sits on the horizon like a gigantic overturned bowl.

Timmun tells us this round mountain is the site of the fire pit, a place of great celebration at winter solstice. Men and women gather here, each building an igloo around the base of this landmark. Because winter ice never forms here, it is accessible from across many seas. Inuit come together at this spot at the same time each winter from many places in the Arctic.

This Land Is Alive

Our sea voyage continues. Flocks of black guillemots swoop and swirl, boasting bits of white on their black wings. A string of eider ducks flaps by. A sleek, whiskered ring seal pops up its head in front of our boat. Within the reflection of land, sea, and sky, we feel so connected to the rhythms of waves, the birds, and the animals in this land of light. But no lingering — we must move on. It will take several hours more to reach our campsite.

Polar Bears!

Here and there, pockets of snow and ice remind us that we are traveling over the frozen top of our planet. On our way, we even observe a few pieces of white ice floating in the dark water ahead. When we get close we see that they are moving swiftly toward land. Recognition comes: three polar bears are swimming right beside us, hurrying! Ears laid back, they paddle straight for the rocky shoreline. The white giants clamber out of the water, rivulets streaming from their massive bodies. Still dripping, the polar bear clan quickly retreats inland.

Jamisee aims his rifle. Sharp words from his mother stop him. "Do not shoot!" Kristiina explains that it is not a good time to hunt these bears. The mother bear is bringing her two-year-old cubs out from inland where she has raised them. After teaching them all the skills needed to survive by the sea, she will leave her cubs to fend for themselves. It is nearly time for the young bears to venture out alone.

Iqalulik

The bears disappear from sight and we move on. Soon Kristiina points out another inuksuk, looking down from the edge of a steep purple-gray slope. This one marks a fishing ground. We have reached our destination — Iqalulik, "place of many fish." We will make our camp here, in the shadow of the ancient signpost.

Welcome to Nunavut

Wearing our survival suits.

The polar bears head inland.

Polar Bear Sighting

The living land gracefully
shows me one of her
many faces.

Timmun tends to our dinner.

Day 4: Setting Up Camp

Iqalulik, "place of many fish," is a perfect spot for our campsite: a hidden piece of level ground in a quiet, peaceful bay. The site is split by a clear mountain stream trickling into the Arctic Ocean. The Silver Dolphin and the freighter canoe are anchored out in the bay, the kayak sits on land.

Energized, we set up three dome tents, securing our tie ropes with a ring of heavy boulders. They look like colorful igloos. Next, we work together to put up our common cook tent. It is a large traditional Inuit summer tent made of white canvas. The wide border skirt is held down by large rocks that we slide into place, creating a traditional tent ring. The central posts that hold up the tent were forgotten back in Kinngait, so Timmun easily makes a new set using some driftwood from along the shore. Last but not least, our portable toilet is set up around the corner behind some large rocks.

Survival Lessons

Nonchalantly, Timmun and Jamisee bring out five rifles and lean them up against a huge boulder. Liz and I receive a quick gun lesson. "Here's the trigger. Pull it if a polar bear comes near, we have loaded the chambers.

I celebrate our new home by building an inuksuk.

Aim upward into the sky and start shouting loudly to scare the bear away. If you walk out of sight of the camp, always take a gun with you."

After obtaining permission from Timmun, I build an innunguaq (inuksuk shaped like a human) near our tents. Jamisee calls out to show us the fresh caribou tracks on the mossy clumps that surround our camp. Kristiina portions out bits of crisp freshly picked sorrel. While we snack on the bittersweet red stems and heart-shaped green leaves, she prepares our dinner. Suddenly we feel very hungry!

We gather around the camp stove and take pleasure in the good meal and good company. But our supply of food will only last another day or two, then we'll need to find more.

Enthralled with our new home, Liz and I explore as afternoon settles into evening. We stay within hearing and seeing range of our guides; after all, we know there are at least three polar bears in the neighborhood. We find many inuksuit, all marking places where life's necessities are met. Here a stone marker leads to a safe pathway. There, another shows a good place to fish. Another marks a cache to store food. A carefully balanced trio of rocks indicates a recently used campsite nearby. More circles of stone indicate places where others have pitched their tents before us.

We head back to camp where Timmun helps us prepare our rods for morning fishing. That job done, we go to our tents, taking our guns with us. I fall asleep, rifle at my side.

Snack time!

Timmun shows us circles of stones where others have pitched tents before us.

Riches of the Arctic Ocean

The land and sea are full
of life.

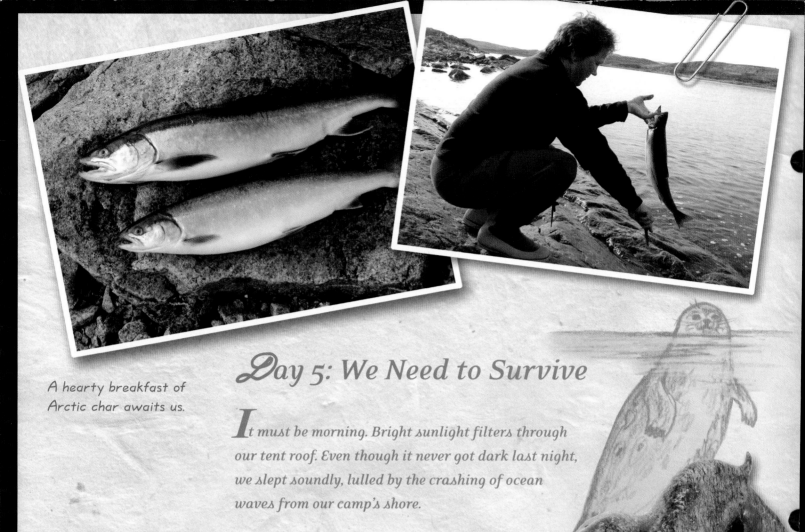

A hearty breakfast of
Arctic char awaits us.

A splash of color in
this rocky landscape.

Day 5: We Need to Survive

*It must be morning. Bright sunlight filters through
our tent roof. Even though it never got dark last night,
we slept soundly, lulled by the crashing of ocean
waves from our camp's shore.*

I step out of our tent and spot Timmun at the
water's edge. He casts, and pulls in a silvery
flash from the ocean. Nearby, at the mouth of
a giant river, stands the inuksuk that marks a
good place to fish. Timmun and Jamisee were out very early and have
already landed two Arctic char for our morning meal. We enjoy a hearty
breakfast, cooked over an open fire. Timmun and Jamisee tell us that
today we are going to hunt caribou. We need food that will keep our
bodies strong for this trip.

After breakfast we climb aboard the freighter canoe, which takes us
out to the *Silver Dolphin* waiting for us in the bay. We're heading out to
sea, to a peninsula where our hunters believe they will find caribou.

Finding Caribou

At our destination, we step out on the stone shore. Majestic mountains
are the powerful backdrop to the sunlight flickering across a rainbow of
Arctic flowers sprouting from this improbable soil.

Jamisee is a good provider. The hard Arctic environment means that hunters must be smart and agile to survive.

Timmun stays near the shore to keep watch by the boats, while Jamisee heads inland to seek our food. Our remaining trio investigates the miracle of the tiny plants that thrive here. Sheltered rock crevices and a perpetual layer of lichens and mosses provide microclimates for delicate and brightly colored flowers.

Where Is Jamisee?

Jamisee has been gone for some time. Scanning the horizon, we see him in the far distance. He is standing atop a mountain, beside an inuksuk that marks a good spot to hunt caribou. I blink and wonder: which is Jamisee? Which is the inuksuk? I know as soon as he disappears.

After several hours he finally comes back. The hunt was unsuccessful. It is time for us to head back to our camp, empty-handed.

But on our return trip, the sharp eyes of our hunters remain ever vigilant. I jump when I hear a loud pop. Our boat suddenly slows and turns around. Jamisee leans over the water and pulls out a ring seal. It lies peacefully in our boat as we pick up speed and continue on. A physical life has been lost, but Kristiina clarifies how the seal offers its life so that her family can have waterproof kamiks (boots) for the winter, her qulliq stone lamp can have oil, and her dogs can have food and strength to pull the winter sleds. I look over at the sleek fur of the seal and see the animal in a different way.

A lone seagull flies over our camp.

37

Living on the Land

Our campsite offers shelter and safety in a vast landscape.

Skillfully following the tracks of a young caribou buck, Jamisee and Timmun make sure that we will eat tonight.

Day 5: We Are Hungry

The inuksuk I built to mark our campsite.

Back at camp, we share thin soup heated over the cook stove. I notice three white stone markers. They point the way to the spot where we cached the seal. Our cairn is covered with a layer of tightly stacked protective stones. The inuksuit that mark our pathways are becoming familiar, like old friends.

Our adventures this morning have left us all tired. After lunch, Liz and I return to our tent. As I drift off to sleep, I think about how I'm beginning to feel like I belong in this place where the ancestors of my Inuit friends walked thousands of years ago.

Wake Up!

There is a loud bang. I startle awake. I sit up at the sound of another bang. A third burst of sound, and I am alert. So is Liz. Alarmed, we scramble out of our tent. Kristiina and Timmun join us.

Inland, on top of a far-off hill, stands Jamisee, waving his arms back and forth. We pull on our boots, grab our guns, and set out in the direction of the shots.

Jamisee is no longer anywhere to be seen. A few lonely inuksuit mark the route we follow.

Moving quickly over the inland meadows, we catch a glimpse of many caribou hoof prints along the way. We hike for more than an hour, winding our way over hills, across bogs, through mossy swamps, and around bright puddles.

At last, in the valley below, we recognize a bright red hood. Jamisee is there with his caribou. He has already skinned, quartered, and packed it for the journey home. The caribou is a lone buck. We are grateful for what the land has offered us once again.

Exhausted yet joyful, our expedition party travels home with our prized tuktu (caribou).

A Long Way Back

Liz and I are given a front shoulder to lug home. Kristiina is our lookout. She carries the gun and adjusts our packs as needed. Carting the food back to camp is an arduous task. If we need to put our load down to rest, we can do so only on mossy tundra; not on sand or stone because that will ruin the meat.

On our long hike back, we pass a curved string of stones. Jamisee identifies it as a caribou hunting blind, a place where his ancestor hunters lay hidden as they waited patiently for the caribou to come. Finally, with aching arms and legs, we approach our tents, now silhouetted against the sparkling evening inlet.

Under the cooling evening sky, Jamisee puts on his fur-lined parka. Near to the hazy hills and the rolling waves, he builds a brand new stone cairn to store the precious caribou meat. Close by stand the fish and seal caches. A raven circles overhead as Jamisee closes in the treasure with a last carefully fitted stone.

Jamisee closes up the food cache to keep our tuktu safe.

Caribou Inuksuk

The power of the ancient land is unfolding; I understand that this caribou has given its life so that we may live.

42

Day 6: The Place of Many Inuksuit

Another new day! Will we finally be going to Inuksugassait (place of many inuksuit)? The most ancient archaeological site in Canada's eastern Arctic, it is a place shrouded in magic and mystery, with relics dating back over four thousand years.

The weather seems perfect for traveling. The morning sky is clear with just a few soft white clouds. A gentle wind ripples the smooth water. Just to be sure, Kristiina checks the weather by satellite phone, and all is well. We fill water bottles from our mountain stream and board the boats, bringing along tuktu (caribou meat) and bannock (flat flour bread). We set out for Inuksugassait.

The *Silver Dolphin* carries us north, up and around the shores of Seekuseelak (the Foxe Peninsula on the southwest side of Baffin Island). My eager heart is pounding. At long last we are approaching Inuksuk Point. As we round the long narrow point I am overwhelmed by my first glimpse of a long rock spit standing alone in the vast ocean, strung with an endless array of inuksuit.

Silent Stone Messengers

I swing myself over the edge of the boat. Awed by the spectacular sight before me, I eagerly stride toward the many ancient inuksuit. Step by step, I approach the legion of silent messengers. What are they trying to tell me? I quiet myself and try to listen for their story.

I am awed by these ancient, silent stones.

Suddenly a mist descends. My vision blurs. I hear Kristiina's voice calling. A fog is rushing in, surrounding us. Timmun and Kristiina warn us that we must leave immediately. It is no longer safe. Reluctantly, I move toward the voices of my guides. Liz calls my name, reaching out to me. We link arms as she urges me on, trusting our guides' voices to lead us to the boat. Kristiina finds us and firmly pulls us forward.

"Get in the boat, be quick! It is time to go! NOW!"

Our hands meet Jamisee's and we are quickly pulled into the *Silver Dolphin*. Out of breath and in the boat, I see nothing beyond the end of my outstretched hand. I am afraid. I think Liz is, too. My sister and I sit close to one another. In the quiet of a damp, dark bumpy voyage home I hang on, disheartened and disappointed. There has been too little time here.

Timmun and Jamisee navigate in the stillness. Just when I wonder whether we are totally lost, the gloom that has engulfed us begins to lighten. I can now distinguish whitecaps as they lurch up from the black ocean below. I feel seasick.

"Look!" shouts Liz. "We are home. Are you OK?"

At last we are back at our camp, safe. I am drained, yet at the same time, restless to return to Inuksugassait. I retreat to my sleeping space where unseen stone people haunt my dreams.

Our campsite shrouded in fog.

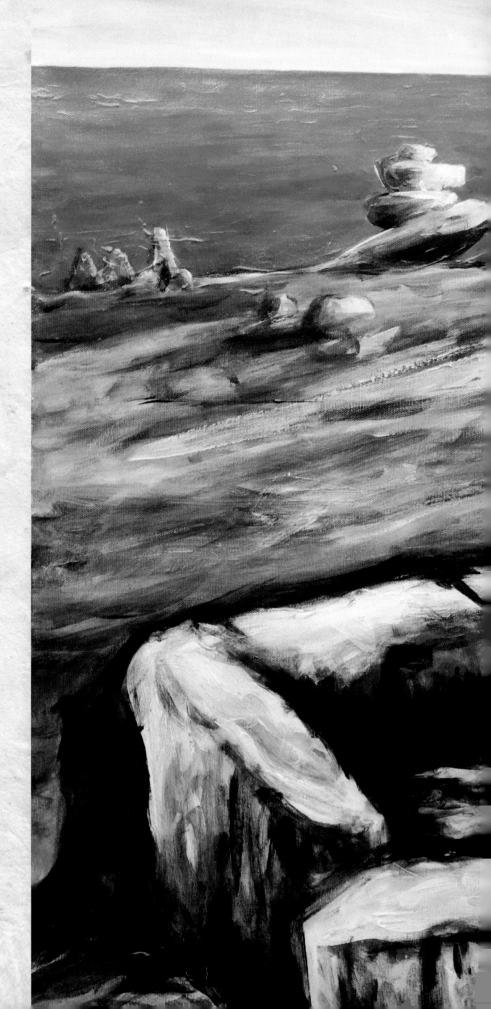

Messages in Stone

Silent stone messengers reflect the need for home, food, balance, beauty, and connection to the Arctic land, sea, and sky.

Day 7: Connections to the Past

*T*immun *and Kristiina inform us it is safe to travel today. We will try once more to explore Inuksugassait.*

Surrounded by silent stone messengers.

With excitement, we board our boat. Jamisee steers us through the choppy waters of the deep indigo sea. As we approach Inuksugassait once again, silhouettes of stone sentinels stand alert, patiently waiting. A lone raven flies overhead as we step ashore.

My companions explore further ahead, while I turn toward a grouping of many inuksuit. Rising from the center, a spectacular inuksuk holds her hundreds of stones in exact balance. Proud and tall, she invites me to make an offering, as many travelers have done before me. I respectfully reach into my pocket, pull back the wrapper, and place half of my energy bar within her vault. Is this silly? It feels right to me.

How many hundreds – or thousands? – of inuksuit are here? Each one has its own message. I stop and look at the inuksuk closest to me. Is this pile of rocks welcoming me? The next inuksuk draws my attention. A message seems to rise from it: "Do not fear, you are not alone. This is a perfect place. It is here that we have lived, loved, hunted, and feasted on this land, plentiful with fish, seal, whale, and caribou."

Ancient Wisdom

Timmun tells us, "These inuksuit have been built by the people who lived here and have spent a long time here. This point of land is practical for the hunting way of life."

Kristiina continues, "These stones tell the story of life here. Many of these inuksuit are stands for drying clothes and fish. Some are directional inuksuit. Some are made for kayak rests. Look, there is a cache beside that tent ring. Look around and you can see how an entire community can live here."

I discover that this is a Thule site from a thousand years ago. The story of this community unfolds. It was a whole Thule village with many stone homes, some built into natural rock faces. Everywhere there are caches, largest for whale, smaller for caribou, seal, walrus, and Arctic char. A twin stone stack shows how a skin kayak was dried. Directional inuksuit point the way to significant destinations. Others withhold their secrets.

The Changing Land

Once again, a mist begins to descend. Like the ancestors have done before us, our group gathers to sip a warm cup of tea. A brisk breeze nips at our faces, and the horizon darkens. It is time to depart.

Rocked by a ruthless sea on the rough ride home, I ponder this land. Every moment changes: wind shifts, sun dims, clouds materialize, sky sprinkles. "Be alert." A little harp seal pops its head up from the water. "Be prepared." A bowhead whale breaches, and next, a pod of belugas swims by. "Expect change. Be ready. Don't waste energy worrying about what's next."

We make it back to camp, climb ashore, and draw together around our evening meal. Amused, we watch a small, soundless Arctic fox raid our seal cache. He has managed to drag the seal skin out. He sees us and boldly pulls harder, finally giving up and disappearing just behind our cook tent. Our attention turns to the raven silently sliding into our caribou cache – and stealing some of our prized tuktu fat!

Inside the remains of an ancient Thule home.

Timmun shares his knowledge of the ancient people on this land.

49

Finding Our Way

By looking through the
sighting hole in this
directional inuksuk,
to the other aligned to
its center, we are shown
the safest route to take
by sea.

Day 7: Food Tastes Better When Shared

The sun settles into the evening, and we work together to prepare our final feast. Timmun gathers stones and constructs an outdoor fireplace.

Jamisee splits a thin layer from a large flat stone slab and lays it across the top of the fireplace. Liz and I are sent to gather fuel: Arctic heather with its high oil content to make the fire burn hot. Kristiina slices tuktu with her ulu.

Crisp fat sizzles across the hot top stone as strips of tuktu meat are carefully placed side by side. Drawing together around the stone stove, we enjoy a traditional banquet of fried caribou. Our food tastes better shared. The ancestors feasted here a millennium ago in this same way under this same sky.

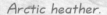

Arctic heather.

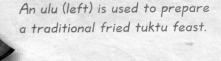

A Busy Day Ahead

Tomorrow is our last day on the land. Jamisee will rise early to fish for Arctic char. We promise to help him to clean and fillet the catch. The fish will be brought back and divided fairly: one third to Jamisee as hunter, one third to Timmun and Kristiina as parents, and one third to Jamisee's wife's parents.

We learn that we will leave at high tide tomorrow. First thing tomorrow, we must pack up our site and ensure that we leave the spot as pristine as when we first arrived.

An ulu (left) is used to prepare a traditional fried tuktu feast.

Goodbye to the Land

The sky becomes softer as the sun lowers and a lovely golden light illuminates our campsite. We hear the haunting cries of loons calling to each other. Mist from the quickly cooling air temperature rises from the Arctic Ocean as the hills across the inlet disappear from sight.

Liz grabs me by the arm and pulls me closer to camp. Timmun helps us prepare our rods for morning fishing. We plan to go to the river mouth at dawn to catch our breakfast.

And then it's time to say goodnight. We retire to our dome tents, taking our guns with us, for the last time.

I look out at the dancing sunset sky. It frames a small inuksuk that marks our Iqalulik campsite and food cache.

Softly, I say goodbye to the seas where Sedna, the mythical Inuit woman of the waves, dwells. I say goodbye to the richness of life she has given to this place: the seals, the fish, the walrus, the whales. Goodbye to the beautiful top of the world. Liz puts my thoughts into her own words: "Thank you for giving us so much, for sharing the goodness of our land."

We sleep soundly that night under the midnight sun.

At the Campfire

We spend our last night on the land, full of food and memories.

We leave Iqalulik behind.

Day 8: Homeward Bound

High tide is coming, so we hustle to pack up camp. Kristiina collects a bucket of seaweed to bring home, a delicacy for later. Our gear piled high, we walk across the gravel path toward our boats. Jamisee and his freighter canoe ferry the supplies back and forth to Timmun and the **Silver Dolphin** out in the bay.

At last, we set out across the sparkling water. Gazing out on the endless landscape, we occasionally see an inuksuk along the skyline to show us where people have been. As we whiz across the waves, Kristiina points out the mountain where we searched for caribou. The land has become familiar. I understand that it is not an empty land, but a land of plenty.

We go by an island that looks like a body in repose. If I could sing a traveling song like the ancestors once did, I would sing:

Aya-yait!

The land is wise,
and powerful.
Like an old friend,
we respect her,

*lest she not share
her secrets.
We need to know the
wrinkles in her valleys,
each ridge upon her hills,
her breath between the clouds,
her tender meadow sigh,
her salty ocean tears.*

*Unless we honor her,
we will be alone,
we will be lost.*

Jamisee's catch is laid out to
take home and divvy up.

This week has been so full of life in response to the land. My heart, mind, and soul feel linked to the passing land, ever changing as it rises in and out of the water.

The Lady of Cape Dorset

Kristiina directs our gaze, "Look, we are almost back in Kinngait." We arrive at low tide. Glad to have our rubber boots, we jump into the shallow waters off shore. Leaving our gear out on the boat until the tide brings her in, we stride ashore.

Back at our beach house, Liz and I wave to Kristiina, Timmun, and Jamisee as they head off to rejoin the rest of their family. Before long we have showered, put on fresh clothes, loaded up the washer and dryer, and turned on the electric lights. It's funny, at camp, we felt wonderful. Now we almost can't believe that we had no flush toilets, showers, or baths. Our only running water was the mountain stream with fresh cold water.

We relax on the sofa and gaze through the window at the view across Telliq Inlet. And there, for the first time, I actually see the lovely Lady of Cape Dorset, as the land herself, lying on her side. There is her head, her shoulder, her abdomen, the curve of her hips. I am finally able to see that signature mountain silhouette that tells travelers they have arrived. We watch the sun gracefully sink to sit beside her.

The Lady of Cape Dorset

Back in Kinngait, I look across at the landform of low mountains across Telliq Inlet and am surprised that I finally see the lovely Lady of Cape Dorset.

A family gathering.

Day 8: The Last Night

We have been invited to Kristiina's home for dinner. As we amble along the village road we are greeted with smiles and nods. I buy some small carvings from local artists. The soapstone was mined from a nearby mountain.

Before long, the howls of Kristiina's sled dogs greet us. Inside, we are introduced to daughters, sons-in-law, grandchildren, and family guests. We all sit down at the family table for a superb dinner of tuktu roast, complete with crowberries for dessert.

Intrigued, we watch Kristiina grind sphagnum moss roots, then twist with arctic willow fluff to make a wick. Next, she pours oil into a shallow carved soapstone container and lights the wick placed along its edge. The qulliq, traditional Inuit lamp, sheds its comforting warmth and light in the center of this Inuit home, just as it has done for thousands of years before.

Past and Present

After dinner, two young women, Maava and Nakasuk, stand, face each other very closely, and begin to make curious resonant noises. Deep breathy sounds and rhythms vibrate between them; their lips do not move. Mesmerized, I watch as they hum, buzz, whirr, drone, and click at each other. Nakusak loses her breath, then starts to giggle.

We learn that throat singing is a game passed down from the elders. Long ago, when it was winter and the men were away hunting, the women invented a game to relieve loneliness and worry. The game consists of imitating joyful sounds: the wind, the birds, animals, people working, running, dogs pulling a fast sled. The challenge is to see who can go the fastest for the longest period of time. Whoever laughs first loses. Although they stand close together, face to face, they do not look at each other because if they do, they start to laugh.

Laughing and clapping follow. Gentle conversation flows around the soft glow of the qulliq. There is some discussion about the Inuit way of life, past and present — about how the traditional way of life has been taken; how the power in people has gone; how power must be welcomed back; how healing and happiness must return.

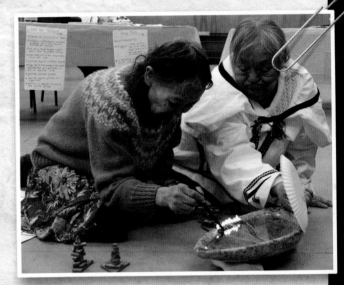

Traditional lighting of the qulliq.

Strolling home under the sweeping strokes of the painterly sky, Liz and I talk about the wonder of spending a week on the land in the traditional way. This was truly a once-in-a lifetime trip, one that took us to ancient places of the land and the heart. I have many thoughts as I reflect on change, culture, and our connection to each other. Tomorrow we fly back to our cities and families and homes, carrying the imprint of all we have met, and all we have experienced at the top of the world.

Singing Sky

With its ancient sacred
stories, this powerful,
patient, and gentle land
embraces me. Reluctantly,
I bid her farewell.

Index